Surrendered

Emma Chester

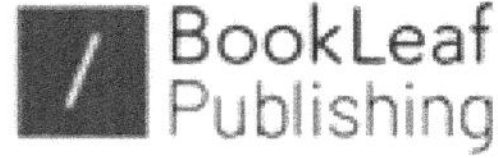

BookLeaf
Publishing

Presentation by *BookLeaf Publishing*

Web: www.bookleafpub.com

E-mail: info@bookleafpub.com

ISBN: 9789357213516

First edition 2023

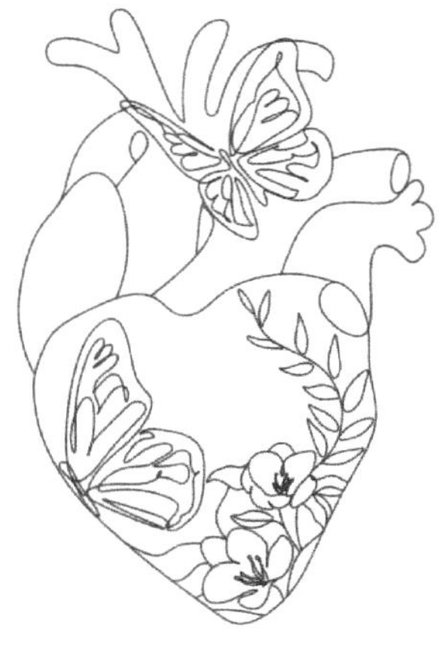

The story behind

Surrender...

One of my favourite things to do in the world is try and control a situation. I want perfection. But life, as you may very well know, is not perfect - and neither are we. We are imperfect people, purposefully broken, so that a perfect God can put us back together. That is the journey that I wanted to tell through these poems: that there is a purpose in our pain, a precious value to our pieces, and that when we fully surrender our lives to the Lord, the rest will follow.

That is also why this story gets told in the order that it does: we must first surrender our hearts to the Lord and allow Him to do a work in us, so that we can surrender ourselves to the ever-changing rhythms He plants in our lives. And it's there, in the surrender, that the Lord allows us to open our hearts up to more. More of Him, more of life, and more of love.

This collection of poems is an out-pouring of the more, and a testament to God's work in my life.

Enjoy! – Emma

Surrendering to the Lord

Little Light

Coffee stained pages,
Tear stained heart.
It's hard to find light,
In all of this dark;
Because the pages burn,
And the memories fade,
But I pray that you won't slip away.
Because with you the coffee doesn't seem so
bitter,
And the light doesn't seem so dark,
The pages don't burn,
Nor do the memories fade.
When I'm with you the world seems right,
Thank you for being just a little light.

Faith

Lead me out to where my feet can't reach, Take
me out upon the open sea,
Where you perfect love is all I need,
And teach me how to run.
Run across a breaking wave,
Where I can raise up my hands and say:
The simple faith,
Is all I need,
You say, "trust in me".
A perfect love, in perfect peace,
The kind of faith I truly need,
Take me deeper than I've ever seen,
Cause you are all I really need.

Have Your Way

I tried to control, my body and mind,
Only to see, I just fall far behind.
Trembling and weak I know that I'm done,
Father, tell me where else can I run?
You open your arms, with the promise of grace,
Now I know that I'm finally safe.
Surrendering everything,
You just want love,
Now all I can ask, is that you will come:
Come live inside of me, like only you can,
Bring forth a fire that the world can't withstand,
Power of pain and sin and defeat,
They're no match for my God in me.
So, I say, have your way…

New Love

I weeped to my mother,
I questioned the Lord,
Little did I know, He was there at the door.
Waiting for me to come running to Him,
Man it feels good to be home again.
Cause I've been fighting your love for a lifetime
too long, All the world's ways now seem so
wrong,
Finally, I have found peace in your arms,
Father, my Savior, forever I'm yours.

Coming Home

All these mistakes I made in pursuit of avoiding
you, Never really let me trust in you,
Went my own way time and again,
Wondering can I now come back in?
Lost like a child, desperate for home,
Always running, got so alone.
Hurting and broken,
My Father I'm here.
Down on my knees,
I need you again.
So many wrongs made in running to you,
You wipe every tear and let me come in,
Father it feels good to be home again.

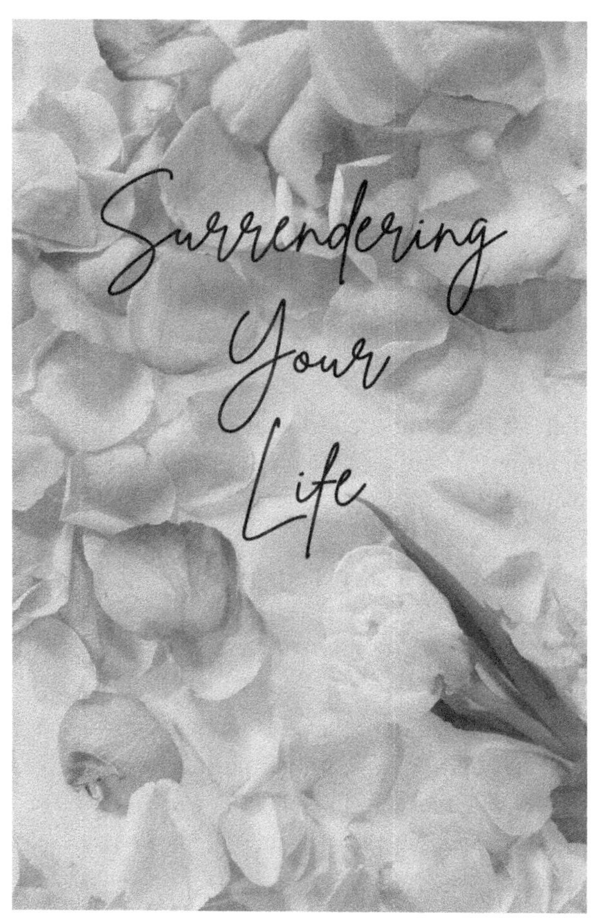
Surrendering
Your
Life

Let Them In

You know, there's gonna be someone who is
utterly infatuated with you. You do get that,
right?
They're going to want to know everything:
Your middle name,
your favorite color,
the cartoons you used to watch growing up on
Saturday mornings. No more of this half
wanted,
Half wasted,
Limelight of a locker room love.
Really know you,
Have you,
Hold you.
And you're going to have to let them in.
You're going to have to compromise on that
unyielding fear that they'll walk away, because
holding back isn't how someone learns your
heart.
You must bare your soul in order for it to be
known,
even if that means breaking it;
Even if it means they walk away.
Because they won't.

That's the thing about those people that have the
insatiable desire to learn your every thought and
feeling:
they don't walk away.
Despite the good, bad, or ugly, they stay.
It's that little bit of fearless,
The tiny ounce of instantaneous courage,
The screaming into the abyss that you're not
afraid:
That is where you learn about yourself.

Say Yes

A paper-thin dress,
My head on your chest.
Who would have thought of the night we'd say
yes?
Cutting through the night like we are learning to
scream,
I have everything when you are looking at me.
I'll steal your heart,
And you'll steal the show.
Who would have thought of our limit's
unknown?
Falling in love beneath the burning stars,
I've thought of a million ways to your heart.
A thief on the prowl,
a hunger for life,
Dropping our weapons,
we are done with this strife.
Who knew all along that you were looking for
me?
I just knew I'd be the last one to leave.
And you, you don't know what to do.
With the spunky little blonde, who stands no
taller than five foot two.

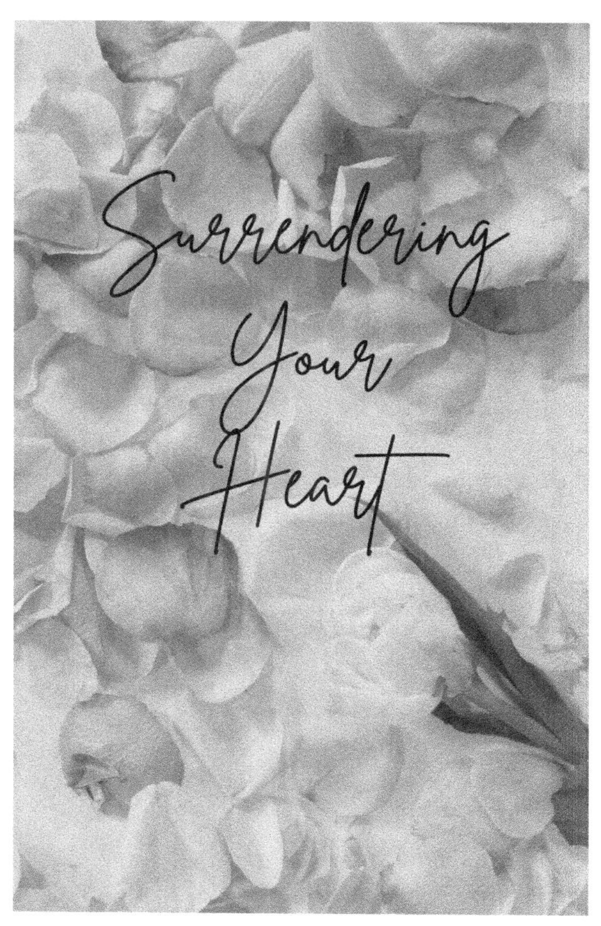
Surrendering
Your
Heart

I've always loved you

I want you to know every beautiful rhythm of
my soul:
Of the girl who couldn't let the world in,
And the boy who embraced it with open arms.
Lost in the sound of our intertwining hearts,
It never seemed to be too much to give myself to
you.
Every fractured piece:
You took them and made them a masterpiece.

Because until now I searched for you,
In between every line,
Holding a bated breath as if it could give you
yours.
Like maybe when our lips finally touched,
The sparks would set fire to the world around us.
I looked for constellations,
And full moons,
And eclipses of the sun,
To tell me that you were mine.
When all along,
All I really needed,
Was your hand in mine.

Finally, home,
You by my side:
A gentle peace resting deep inside.
Lips I've longed for,
For a lifetime too long.
Every answered prayer found in your arms.

Where do you go when you're scared?

Who do you find in a crowded room?
Whose arms, are you gonna fall in to?
When you're drunk on life and running scared,
Who do you know that will always be there?
Because then I think I'd know who to choose.
Then I think I'd know that it's always been you.
Cause when I'm lost in the dark and I can't see,
I know that you'll always be there for me.
When I'm wandering the world like a long lost
soul,
I know it's your hand that I need to hold.
Because if I were drunk in a crowded room,
You'd be the arms I hope I choose.

Change Makers

You and I,
We are creators.
Cataclysmic change makers.
The doers and thinkers that will change the
world, If we don't burn it down first.
You and I,
We build from nothing.
The passions that consume us come out,
And darling it is art;
It is terror and beauty and every spectacular
thing, An infinite world of infinites at our finger
tips.
If we fool around we just might make something
of ourselves. An accident of artistry.
That's what they'll call us.
And it,
Will be wonderful.

Dancing Time

Hey honey let's go dancing,
An all night long romancing,
A softly swaying through the streets where we
don't plan on staying.
Hey honey let's start moving,
A softer kind of grooving,
A pick your feet up and learn to love the
speakers booming.
Don't want to ever stop,
No matter what we've got,
Just want to feel your hand in mine.
Because baby, I do believe that,
It's dancing time.

My Soldier

He tasted of gun powder and healing hearts,
Like the sunshine first creeping in the window in
an early morning, And a cool breeze filtering
through the trees.
He felt like coming home to something new,
And instantly memorizing every corner and
crevice. He was a soldier of solitude,
Used to waging war on the world alone:
A martyr to the mayhem for the sake of love.
"No more, my dear"
I would tell him sweetly,
Pink lips parting in a promise of forever.
No more must you walk alone in the life we
love,
Now I shall follow you to whatever end we
meet,
A fearless fate we will face,
So long as I'm yours.

That's how you know

You ask me, how is it that I love him?
And I tell you, how could I not?
When he makes falling feel like flying,
And my heart feel like it might burst.

Let's Get Lost

Hey,
Can we get lost among the lights?
The lights and the lies and the lull of laughter.
Let's follow the frat boys down forbidden allies
and let's laugh too loudly and let the world
judge.
We can take the top down and take the
backroads, and maybe by the time the sun comes
up we will have had enough.
Maybe then I'll be sick of you,
Or sick on you…
Sick on life and love and luck.
Can we wander streets of foreign cities and sip
every fabulous thing?
Even if it scares you, let's do it anyways.
Let's skip the street signs and go straight for the
road,
Charting a path that is all our own.
I want to make you uncomfortable,
I want you hopped up and high and horribly
honest.
Tell me secrets till your throat hurts and my
heart is full,
Take me away from this reality we so despise.
Can we pretend this day never has to end?

Did you know I'd go down with you?

Those dandelion flowers,
And your hands against my back.
I knew I had it all,
When I heard the sound your laugh.
Those crystal rushing waters,
Your lips crash into mine,
I knew this was a day,
I could live in for all time.
Cause you have this special power,
You hold it over me,
That when I am beside you,
There's no one else I see.
And you take me to a place that,
Leaves room for just me and you,
And now I'm going down,
With the sinking ship of you.
Down, down, down we go into the blue.
After the echo, of me and you.
We will follow that echo till the end of time,
Because yours is a voice,
That I know as well as mine.
There will be no need for air,

When my heart is next to yours,
Because within the echo,
The world can never hurt.
So now we go on down,
With the sinking ship of us,
Down straight to the bottom,
So our hands can finally touch.
And I'll think of all the flowers,
That I picked along the way,
When your hands touched my body,
And I memorized your face.
Hold on to your power,
Cause my love we still have time.
Deep within the echo, you always will be mine.

You were never broken to me

They say "damaged goods" is printed across
your forehead like a warning label,
Telling me to keep my distance.
But what if I told you I never learned how to
read?
Or that I was willing to simply ignore the
caution tape you had wrapped around your heart.
That I was trained to climb mountains,
So reaching the peak of your heart wouldn't be
hard,
It doesn't matter how far I have to climb.
The murder of your love is nothing to a detective
like me,
I make my work in crime and trust me,
I've seen worse.
You think you are damaged beyond repair,
They think you need fixing,
But what if they were wrong?
How would you feel if I told you that perhaps,
What I need in life is a little damage.

A gentle kind of love

Tender,
My defender…
Just know I won't let go,
Cause now I've found my home,
It's sentimental.
In the dark of the night,
You are a shining light,
Remember:
Your weakest sparks,
Can reignite my heart,
A love that burns so deep,
Is taking over me,
And I'll surrender….
You feel gentle:
Tender.

My Muse

Now how do I tell you that you inspire me?
That every love sick and sappy line I've written
was about you,
The way you make me flutter,
The way our flirtation has only fanned my
flame.
How do I say that you ignite me?
Your touch like a match,
Your words like the wind,
I am burning for you.
Watch me turn to ash as I write pages of prose
for the sake of your heart,
That maybe somewhere between the lines,
You will read and find me.
Cowering from the truth,
From my heart,
From the words I dare not breathe aloud.
Because you inspire me,
And sometimes that feels like it shouldn't be
allowed.

Forever Won't be Long Enough

I would love you with a lifetime full of forevers,
Of a breaking, bending, aching heart,
That longs to be held by your hands.
Sweet lips part in the cool night air,
And my darling I am yours.
I am beheld by a beauty so magnificent I might
as well be dust,
Trodden beneath the feet with which you walk.
I'd perish for you my love,
If only to be a glimmer in your mind,
A fading echo shouting into the void of time.
Timeless tales they'd tell of us,
Of fractured hearts and troubled minds.
Insanity, sweet one, never seemed too much a
stretch for you.

Replay

You make me understand why people sing in the
shower.
Why mixtapes get made,
And people are driven mad.
A minute with you is better than a month with
anyone else,
And staring down into your warm brown eyes,
Makes me see how loving someone can be
dangerous.
Why people warn against it and wish the battle
between hearts was not so bloody.
But my god,
They've never tasted your lips.
They've never felt your hands draw lazy circles
across their thighs,
Or how my heart has never been so close to
being obliterated as when I saw you be weak.
That is worth every skipped song, slip in the
shower, saying that things will be better in the
morning,
When they won't.
Not unless you're with me

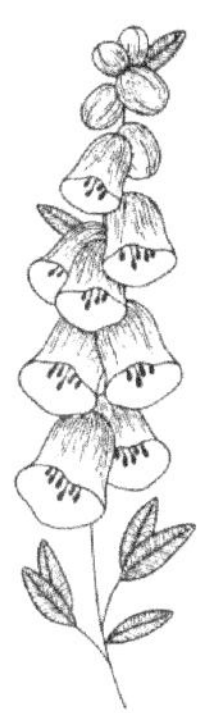# The journey doesn't end here...

Surrendering is something that I will constantly be in pursuit of. It is an ever-changing, ever-growing, and ever-evolving process that we will be attempting to conquer for the rest of our lives.

Our human nature, that fiery will and stubborn independence, will always fight against

submitting to an all-knowing and fully loving
God, because if you're anything like me, that
means giving up control, which is just about the
farthest thing from easy.
So, if you're anything like me, let me be the first
person to tell you to let go anyways.
Do it scared, do it unsure, do it with gradually
unfurling hands that you once held clenched shut
tight, do it because it will leave you a million
times better off than figuring things out on your
own, do it because it's what the Lord calls us to.
Everyone's journey of surrender in life is going
to look different, but that doesn't mean that it is
any less of a journey worth taking. Some of your
chapters may be longer than others, and some
pages may hold tear stains, but within that
surrender there is a new life of passion and
purpose that is unlike anything else that this
world can offer. It is a lifetime of love and joy
that cannot be deterred by human nature or
determined by circumstances. It is the beauty of
Christ's love for us.
It is something I pray over every single hand that
picks up this book.
Thank you for giving me the privilege of being
used as a vessel for the Lord for just a few pages
in your life – you have a beautiful story ahead.
-Emma

www.ingramcontent.com/pod-product-compliance
Lightning Source LLC
Chambersburg PA
CBHW070727160726
48003CB00006BA/2401